Cornerstones of Freedom

Times Square

WENDE FAZIO

CHILDREN'S PRESS®
A Division of Grolier Publishing
New York • London • Hong Kong • Sydney
Danbury, Connecticut

Visit Children's Press on the Internet at:
http://publishing.grolier.com

Library of Congress Cataloging-in-Publication Data

Fazio, Wende.
   Times Square / Wende Fazio.
      p. cm.—(Cornerstones of freedom)
   Includes index.
   Summary: Describes the history of the New York City neighborhood
famous for bright lights and Broadway shows, from its beginnings as
Longacre Square in the early 1800s through its growth, decline, and present-
day revitalization.
   ISBN: 0-516-21184-6 (lib. bdg.)   0-516-26530-X (pbk.)
   1. Times Square (New York, N.Y.)—History—Juvenile literature.
2. New York (N.Y.)—History—Juvenile literature. [1. Times Square (New
York, N.Y.)—History. 2. New York (N.Y.)—History.] I. Title. II. Series.
F128.65.T5F39   1999
974.7`1—dc21
                                                      98-37340
                                                         CIP
                                                         AC

GROLIER
PUBLISHING

Shoppers, workers, and tourists have to scramble for walking space on its crowded New York City sidewalks. As many as seven thousand pedestrians an hour, or about two people per second, pass by any given place. Its streets are crammed with theaters and thunder with traffic. At night, it glimmers more brilliantly than at noon. And an electronic headline sign, called a motogram, wraps around one of its many buildings, spelling out news in moving letters that can be read from several blocks away. This is Times Square.

The latest headlines are shown on the motogram that wraps around this building in Times Square.

Times Square grew up around the area where Broadway, an avenue running diagonally across Manhattan, slashes across Seventh Avenue at 42nd Street. It is the heart of New York's theater district and a colorful focal point of New York City. Because of its bustling streets, rich cultural diversity, and the "X" crossing of Broadway and Seventh Avenue, Times Square is often referred to as the "crossroads of the world." It is well known for the tremendous electrical displays that light up the night, advertising movies, hotels, Broadway shows, and consumer products. But how did Times Square become such a hub of activity?

The story of Times Square starts at the beginning of the 1800s, when most of the settled area of Manhattan was concentrated on the southern tip of the island, where the land meets New York Harbor. It was in these waters in 1524, that the first European, an Italian explorer named Giovanni da Verrazano, sailed and documented his visit to Manhattan Island. Henry Hudson, sailing for the Dutch, also passed through the harbor in 1609, entering what is now called the Hudson River. He was warmly welcomed by the Algonquian, the local Indian tribe. Soon after, Belgian and Dutch settlers began to arrive on the island. In 1624, the Dutch purchased the island from the Indians for the equivalent of $24. In 1674, the Dutch traded Manhattan to the English, and England renamed the territory New York.

Giovanni da Verrazano

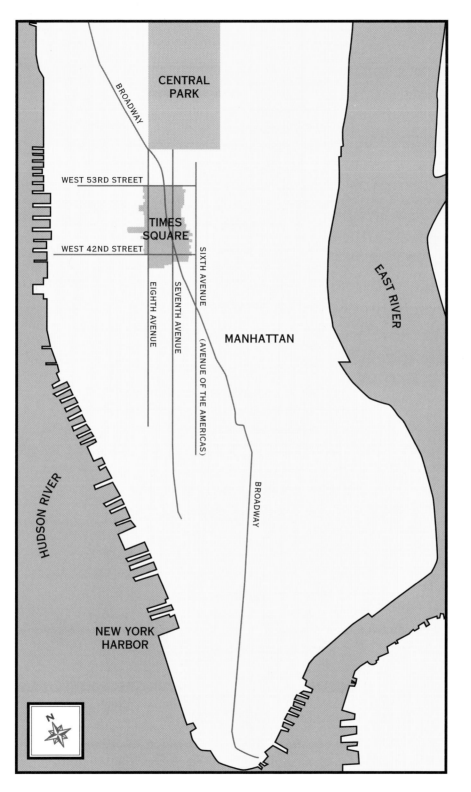

CENTRAL PARK

WEST 53RD STREET

TIMES SQUARE

WEST 42ND STREET

EIGHTH AVENUE

SEVENTH AVENUE

SIXTH AVENUE

(AVENUE OF THE AMERICAS)

BROADWAY

MANHATTAN

EAST RIVER

HUDSON RIVER

BROADWAY

NEW YORK HARBOR

N

Times Square is located on the island of Manhattan, one of New York City's five boroughs.

As the Dutch and the English settled the southern tip of Manhattan, wagon trails and carriage roads were created that traveled north toward the middle of the island and beyond, where small cabbage farms and horse stables were established. This area, which is present-day Times Square, was known as Long Acre and was named after a London neighborhood. The two most traveled of these colonial roadways were today's Broadway and Seventh Avenue. With the exception of a short stay by General George Washington during the American Revolution, Long Acre remained unchanged until the middle of the 1800s.

In 1811, when street engineer John Randall Jr. laid out the gridiron street pattern for Manhattan, the city's population was one hundred thousand.

A view of Long Acre about 1800

By 1850, it had grown to five hundred thousand. By the outbreak of the Civil War in 1861, there were almost one million people. Gradually, as more people created more traffic, Long Acre, which by then was known as Longacre Square, became more developed. Soon commerce replaced the farms and carriage houses. William H. Vanderbilt, grandson of the prominent New York millionaire Cornelius Vanderbilt, owned and managed The American Horse Exchange, located on the square through most of the mid- to late-1800s. (The Exchange was a business that boarded, traded, and sold horses.) Modest houses were built along 42nd Street and by 1853, four separate buildings occupied the square. Two more buildings were built near the square across Seventh Avenue, to the west. Between

The Astors' huge home was located on the corner of 5th Avenue and 65th Street.

1830 and 1860, another prominent New York family, the Astors, built a neighborhood in the Longacre district that remained exclusive until the 1890s. But vacant lots lined the east side of Broadway, from 42nd to 44th streets.

7

Visitors from all over the area came to see the Crystal Palace.

In 1853, after learning of the crowds attracted to the Great Exhibition of 1851 in Hyde Park, London, New Yorkers decided to build their own attraction. New York's Great Exhibition was a World's Fair that celebrated the technology of the day. It took place in the Crystal Palace, a huge structure made of iron and glass. New Yorkers named their exhibition hall after the one in London, and built it on the vacant lots east of Broadway. It was 1,300 feet (396 meters) long, but was still not nearly as large as the one in England. The Latting Observatory, built at the same time, was located directly across the street from the Crystal Palace. The observatory was named after its builder, Warren Latting. From the observation deck, sightseers enjoyed breathtaking views to the west of Broadway.

The Crystal Palace exhibited all-American inventions such as the sewing machine, plows, and a new device, the working elevator. Paintings, fine woods, fabrics, and handicrafts of famous silversmiths were on loan from Europe for display. But some of the attractions were considered gaudy (bright and showy, but lacking in good taste).

Alligators, dancing bears, six-legged calves, a fat woman, and giants were also exhibited.

In 1856, after only three years, the Latting Observatory burned to the ground. In 1858, fire destroyed the Crystal Palace. But while they lasted, both were similar to the present-day carnival atmosphere of Times Square.

The first theater on the square was the idea of a cigar maker and inventor named Oscar Hammerstein (grandfather of the famous songwriter, Oscar Hammerstein II). Hammerstein was also a composer, concert organizer, and businessman.

Before his theatrical career, Hammerstein was a successful inventor. He invented a device that molded twelve cigars at once. It could operate much faster than a single worker molding one cigar at a time. Hammerstein also patented a cigar-rolling machine, a cigar cutter, and an inkwell that closed automatically. (Inkwells were containers for ink, which were needed for writing with pens before ballpoint pens were invented in 1888.)

Using the money he earned from his successful inventions, Hammerstein built opera houses to the north and the south of Longacre Square. Hammerstein then decided to build an entertainment center in the middle of Longacre Square that would be in the carnival tradition of the Crystal Palace.

Oscar Hammerstein

Prior to 1895, most theaters and opera houses were located south of the square. The Bowery district, more than thirty blocks to the south, housed the first of the New York theaters. In 1836, there were a total of six theaters in New York, all filled to capacity every night. Throughout the mid-1800s, theater construction began to slowly spread northward. In 1893, the Broadway Theatre opened at Broadway and 41st Street. But the electric lights of the theaters stopped at 42nd Street, which was then nicknamed Thieve's Lair, because of pickpocketing and other forms of thievery that were common occurrences.

This photograph, taken about 1895, is a view of Thalia Theater, located in the Bowery.

Hammerstein was determined to cross 42nd Street and turn Thieve's Lair into a hub of entertainment. Because of its crossroads location, he believed he could lure audiences from miles away, instead of from just a few blocks away. He purchased eight lots on the east side of Broadway for $1 million.

In 1895, Hammerstein opened the Olympia, which featured three music halls, three theater halls, a roof garden, and a café. The Olympia promised "to be one of the great sights of the [city]," declared *Munsey's* magazine, which ran regular features on New York show business.

In this 1895 photograph, passengers board streetcars in front of Hammerstein's Olympia Theatre.

A view of some of the private boxes inside the Olympia Theatre

The Olympia's music hall occupied the corner of 45th Street. The theater occupied the corner of 44th Street, and the concert hall was located in the center. The music hall had 124 private boxes, special sections of seats that are set off from the rest of the seats in a hall, and are usually reserved for wealthy or important people. According to Hammerstein, the Olympia housed more private boxes than any other music hall in the world. The structure contained automatic sprinklers and was advertised as fireproof. Two massive carved doorways led to a marble foyer from a pillared entrance with twin towers and a passenger elevator. On opening night, ten thousand people paid to get in, even though there was seating for only six thousand.

But the Olympia proved to be too expensive. A steam explosion twelve hours after the opening night festivities killed two employees and seriously burned ten others. A series of theatrical failures bankrupted Hammerstein.

Hammerstein, however, was determined to keep his big dreams for the square alive. Fund-raisers were organized for him by his theatrical and music stars and earned him $8,000. Using secondhand bricks and lumber, he built his next theater, the Victoria, at 42nd Street and Seventh Avenue. Leaving his son, Willie, to manage the Victoria, Hammerstein went on to build the Republic Theatre, next door to the Victoria. Across the top of these two theaters, he constructed the Paradise Roof Gardens, which quickly became a popular tourist attraction.

Visitors dine in the Paradise Roof Gardens in this photograph, taken about 1910.

Adolph S. Ochs

While Hammerstein was busy building theaters and music halls in Longacre Square, another prominent New Yorker, Adolph S. Ochs, was building new headquarters for his internationally known newspaper, the *New York Times,* in the center of the square. Ochs saw the location as a perfect spot to publish and sell his newspaper. In 1902, he purchased the northern three-sided corner of the square.

At the same time, The Interborough Rapid Transit Company was constructing an underground train system (the subway) next to the Times Tower, the name given to the newspaper's headquarters. August Belmont, builder of the subway, wrote the following letter to Alexander E. Orr, president of the Board of the Rapid Transit Commission:

> *No station on our route is liable to be more active or important than that at 42nd Street and Broadway. . . . Owing to the conspicuous position which the* Times *holds, it being one of the leading New York journals, it would seem fitting that the square on which the building stands should be known as Times Square and the station named Times Square Station. Long Acre, the present name of the Square, means nothing, and it is not generally known throughout the city.*

Belmont's idea was brought before the city council and was unanimously approved. On April 13,

1904, Mayor George B. McClellan signed the resolution, and the Times Square legend, a place already famous throughout much of the world, formally began.

The Times Tower building rose 375 feet (114 m), the second-highest building in New York in 1904. The newspaper finished moving all of its heavy presses and equipment from its downtown location to Times Tower on December 31, 1904.

To celebrate the newspaper's formal arrival into Times Tower and Times Square, and to welcome the new year, Ochs staged a huge display of fireworks launched from the top of the tower. The symbol for the old year's passing was a huge, brightly lit globe that slid down a pole on top of the tower. This great show of fireworks started the famous tradition of New Year's Eve celebrations in Times Square and continues today. Within a few years, the *New York Times* left the Times Tower for larger headquarters on West 43rd Street, but nobody would dare change the square's world-famous name.

The Times Tower was one of the two highest buildings in New York during the early 1900s.

W.C. Fields, in costume for one of his vaudeville acts

At the beginning of World War I (1914–18), most theaters had moved to Times Square from the Bowery and Union Square areas. The music business known as vaudeville, dance halls, and cabarets (small restaurants with musical entertainment) were common in these theaters. Perhaps the most popular of these entertainment events was vaudeville. Vaudeville was a variety show of unconnected musical, dancing, comedy, and specialty acts. The shows were affordable entertainment for working people and provided a pleasant escape from their everyday lives.

Vaudeville was different from other forms of entertainment because each performer appeared only once in each show and rarely for more than twenty minutes, no matter how famous or popular they were. As a result of being on stage for such a short time, there was no room for mistakes. Some of America's best-loved comedians, such as W.C. Fields, Bob Hope, and the Marx Brothers, learned their trade in vaudeville.

Other famous talents rose out of the old vaudeville theaters, as well. George M. Cohan was an actor, singer, dancer, playwright, composer, director, and producer who spent all of his life in the theater. As a child, he appeared in his family's vaudeville act, *The Four Cohans*. He was managing the act and writing vaudeville sketches at age seventeen. His first full-length play, *The Governor's Son,* a fast-paced show of songs, comedy, and drama, opened in New York in 1901. *Little Johnny Jones* opened in 1904, and introduced two of Cohan's best-loved songs, "I'm a Yankee Doodle Dandy" and "Give My Regards to Broadway." His all-American World War I songs, "You're a Grand Old Flag" and "Over There," were two of his personal favorites. He took on a serious role as Nat Miller in Eugene O'Neill's *Ah, Wilderness!* which many consider the finest performance of his career. A statue of Cohan that honors his life, talent, and contributions to the theater stands in Duffy Square on 47th Street between Broadway and Seventh Avenue.

George M. Cohan

The Cohan statue in Duffy Square

Four Ziegfeld girls in costume, about 1920

Another popular variety show during Cohan's time was Ziegfeld's Follies. Created by Florenz Ziegfeld to "glorify the American girl," he turned beautifully costumed, carefully chosen "Ziegfeld Girls" into symbols of glamour and elegance. One of his twenty-one annual Follies was held at Times Square in the New Amsterdam Theatre in 1927.

Eugene O'Neill, one of the United States's most famous playwrights, was born in 1888 in a long-gone hotel on Times Square. In 1936, O'Neill was the first American playwright to win the Nobel Prize for Literature.

In 1891, three years before the opening of Hammerstein's Olympia, the American inventor Thomas Alva Edison patented his invention, the kinetoscope. The kinetoscope was a hand-cranked device that projected moving images onto a screen.

On April 23, 1896, the first public presentation in New York of moving pictures occurred at Koster & Bials Music Hall at Herald Square, located ten blocks south of Times Square. It was an instant success. Vaudeville programs began to add these popular devices to their programs in 1899.

Nickelodeons (amusement halls that featured moving pictures and specialized in hand-cranked machines that showed movies to one viewer at a time) became popular entertainment. In 1904, there were no known nickelodeons in Manhattan. By 1907, there were so many that attendance averaged two million people a day. Nickelodeons rarely showed movies on screens to an audience, mainly because that was much less popular. People wanted to watch these short films by themselves. The first and most popular nickelodeons were located downtown. The greatest of them was the Automatic Vaudeville, on 14th Street near Union Square, which had many rows of machines.

This 1907 photograph shows the rows of nickelodeons along the walls inside the Automatic Vaudeville.

As the popularity of the moving picture grew, many of the older vaudeville theaters and music halls were converted into movie theaters. One of the first to convert was the Palace Theatre, at 47th Street and Broadway, once the center of vaudeville. The reason was simple: Live theater, with a maximum of eight performances a week, couldn't compete with the movies, which could show a film at least three or four times daily, seven days a week.

Times Square changed dramatically after the Stock Market Crash of 1929. During the Great Depression, few theaters were built. Many of the existing theaters became movie houses that showed sexually explicit films. Burlesque, shows that featured the display of women's bodies, was introduced. Cheap restaurants, penny arcades, and dime museums soon followed, as well as an increase in prostitution.

At the same time, the American music business had produced more than five hundred thousand songs. Many of those made popular in the Times Square theaters were heard across the country on radio and used in Hollywood films.

By the 1920s, people flocked to theaters along Broadway, including the Palace (right), to see movies.

But the decline of Times Square continued, and was hastened by World War II (1939–45). During the war, many servicemen came to Times Square looking for adult entertainment. The area soon became known for vice (evil actions or habits). The number of cheap rooming houses, hotels, adult bookstores, peep shows, and sex arcades increased.

In spite of Times Square's decline, one thing that did not change was its advertisement displays. Throughout Times Square's history, advertising has been an important part of its fame and notoriety. The huge electric signs that

During the 1940s, huge advertisement displays began lighting up Times Square at night.

make Times Square the heart of the bright-lights district started out small and modest and grew to be enormous and showy. New Yorkers began to advertise as soon as they had a wall on which to hang a sign. Anyone with something to sell nailed a notice over his or her door, or hung a sign above the sidewalk, or painted the word for the available product on the pavement. A cigar shop announced its product with a huge cigar, a locksmith with a large set of keys and saws, a dentist with a mouthful of teeth, and so on.

Soon after gas street lamp lighting came into use in 1814, the street lamps had quickly crept up Broadway. Electric lights followed later. By the beginning of the 1900s, producers and managers in the entertainment field, as well as business leaders, felt that using electric lights would mean they would make more money. The actress Maxine Elliott was the first actress to have her name spelled out in bulbs on the theater on 39th Street where she performed. Many other theaters soon copied the idea and displayed their own stars in even brighter lights.

Laws adopted in 1916 gave Times Square and Broadway special consideration for the size and brilliance of outdoor displays. The only regulation was that the displays could not be too heavy (to prevent them from falling down onto the sidewalks). As a result of having only this one restriction, the lighting displays were built bigger and brighter. Huge crowds filled the square to see them.

These nighttime lighting displays have often been called "the finest free show on Earth." The first moving electric sign in Times Square appeared in 1928. Some of the more famous displays have included 12-inch (30-centimeter) soap bubbles lathering up from a huge bar of soap and floating across Times Square, billowing clouds of steam rising from a cup of coffee the size of a house, and cigarette rings puffed into the air from an open mouth the size of a truck.

Pepsi-Cola erected a series of advertisements, one of which was, at the time, the largest outdoor ad in the world. In 1959, the company constructed the famous Pepsi-Cola waterfall. The display used 20,000 gallons (70,400 liters) of water, 35,000 lightbulbs, and more than one million watts of electricity!

Today, advertising styles have changed. Many of the old signs are gone. The city, however, is trying to preserve this part of its recent past. All new buildings in the area are required to have signs with a minimum amount of brightness—the brighter the better! But the area is in the midst of a massive restoration which will do more to change the neighborhood than anything else since the electric light bulb.

When Pepsi-Cola erected this advertisement on top of a clothing store in the 1940s, it was the largest outdoor ad in the world.

The Walt Disney Company is leading the way in the revitalization efforts for Times Square. The company's first major restoration project has been to renovate the New Amsterdam Theatre, where Ziegfeld's Follies were once performed, as a showcase for its film-based, family-oriented theater productions. Disney will also be a part of the huge hotel and entertainment complex being constructed at the northeast corner of Eighth Avenue and 42nd Street.

Planet Hollywood will be moving its flagship restaurant from midtown to a new entertainment complex to be built on Times Square, which will include a fifty-story hotel with a movie-star theme. The new complex is scheduled for completion in time for the spectacular millennium celebration in Times Square that is planned for New Year's Eve, 1999. Planet Hollywood already operates the

Times Square All Star Café, a restaurant with a sports theme, at Broadway and 45th Street.

On March 1, 1998, the Empire Theatre, located on 42nd Street between Seventh and Eighth avenues, was moved 170 feet (52 m) west, where its original interior will be restored. It will serve as an entrance to a new twenty-five-screen movie complex. The Empire Theatre was built in 1912 and was originally called the Eltinge Theatre. It was named for the actor Julian Eltinge, who was famous for playing female roles. When the Empire first opened, it specialized in comedies with Laurence Olivier and Clark Gable among some of the many featured performers. The comedy team of Bud Abbott and Lou Costello first appeared here in 1931.

Bud Abbott (right) and Lou Costello balloons "pull" the Empire Theatre to its new home along 42nd Street. It took six hours to move the theater 170 feet (52 m).

The Embassy Theatre, located on Seventh Avenue at 46th Street, is also being restored to its former glory. Built in 1925, the Embassy serves as New York City's first large-scale tourist information center and is called the Times Square Visitors Center. It offers tourists Metrocard (subway and bus) sales, tour bus and theater ticket sales, free tourist brochures and directions to restaurants, museums, and events across New York City. Among the many historic details of the Embassy that have been restored are elegant chandeliers and hand-painted murals that were originally designed to satisfy the high-society tastes of the wealthy patrons who attended the silent films of the 1920s.

The Times Square Visitors Center

Times Square will soon be the new backdrop for the ABC-TV news program, *Good Morning, America,* and other news, sports, and entertainment programs. The construction of this new television studio complex is scheduled to be complete in time to broadcast the millennium celebration from Times Square.

Today, Times Square still draws crowds. Whether people come for the bright lights, the Broadway shows, or for Disney, Times Square promises to dazzle and entertain. Times Square is still the crossroads of the world.

A crowd gathers in Times Square to celebrate one of many festivities marking the area's restoration.

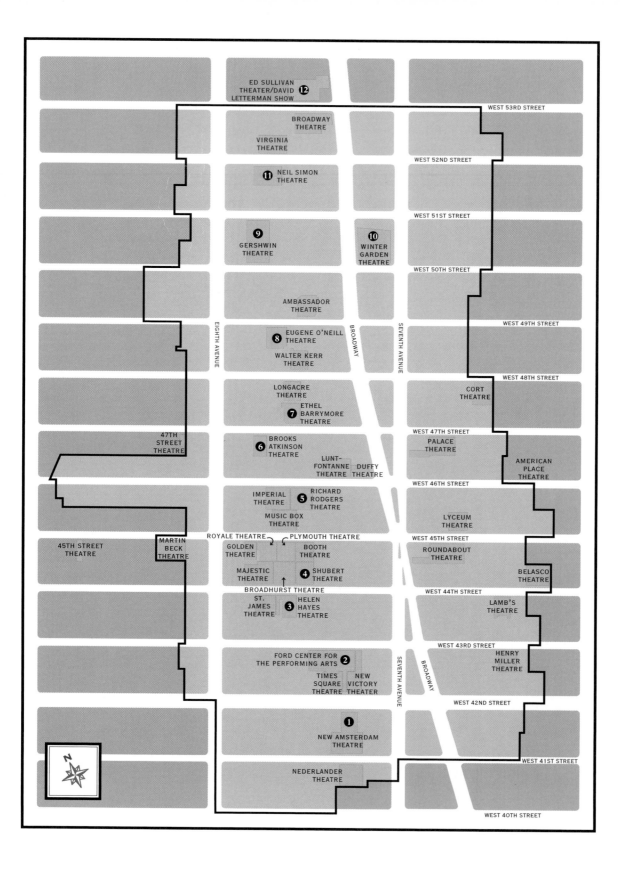

ED SULLIVAN
THEATER/DAVID ❿
LETTERMAN SHOW

WEST 53RD STREET

BROADWAY
THEATRE

VIRGINIA
THEATRE

WEST 52ND STREET

❶❶ NEIL SIMON
THEATRE

WEST 51ST STREET

❾   ❿
GERSHWIN   WINTER
THEATRE   GARDEN
                  THEATRE

WEST 50TH STREET

AMBASSADOR
THEATRE

WEST 49TH STREET

EIGHTH AVENUE

BROADWAY

SEVENTH AVENUE

❽ EUGENE O'NEILL
THEATRE

WALTER KERR
THEATRE

WEST 48TH STREET

LONGACRE
THEATRE

CORT
THEATRE

❼ ETHEL
BARRYMORE
THEATRE

WEST 47TH STREET

47TH
STREET
THEATRE

❻ BROOKS
ATKINSON
THEATRE

PALACE
THEATRE

LUNT-
FONTANNE   DUFFY
THEATRE   THEATRE

AMERICAN
PLACE
THEATRE

WEST 46TH STREET

IMPERIAL   RICHARD
THEATRE   RODGERS
        ❺ THEATRE

LYCEUM
THEATRE

MUSIC BOX
THEATRE

ROYALE THEATRE   PLYMOUTH THEATRE

WEST 45TH STREET

45TH STREET
THEATRE

MARTIN
BECK
THEATRE

GOLDEN   BOOTH
THEATRE   THEATRE

ROUNDABOUT
THEATRE

MAJESTIC   ❹ SHUBERT
THEATRE   THEATRE

BELASCO
THEATRE

BROADHURST THEATRE

WEST 44TH STREET

ST.
JAMES   HELEN
THEATRE ❸ HAYES
         THEATRE

LAMB'S
THEATRE

WEST 43RD STREET

FORD CENTER FOR ❷
THE PERFORMING ARTS

HENRY
MILLER
THEATRE

TIMES   NEW
SQUARE   VICTORY
THEATRE   THEATER

SEVENTH AVENUE

BROADWAY

WEST 42ND STREET

❶
NEW AMSTERDAM
THEATRE

WEST 41ST STREET

N

NEDERLANDER
THEATRE

WEST 40TH STREET

WHAT'S IN A THEATER NAME?

Times Square is the theater capital of the world, where more than forty theaters are located. Many of these historic theaters are named after legends of American theater.

❶ New Amsterdam. The Disney Corporation gave one of Broadway's oldest theaters new life with its recent renovation. "New Amsterdam" was the name of New York City for many years.

❷ Ford Center for the Performing Arts. New theater constructed on the site of the former Lyric Theatre; funded by the Ford Motor Company.

❸ Helen Hayes Theatre. Named for the actress nicknamed the "First Lady of American Theatre." Next door to Sardi's, a legendary Broadway restaurant commonly frequented by celebrities.

❹ Shubert Theatre. Named for Sam Shubert, one of the legendary theater producers from the early 1900s.

❺ Richard Rodgers Theatre. Named for the composer who wrote such musicals as *The Sound of Music* and *Oklahoma!*

❻ Brooks Atkinson Theatre. Named for an influential *New York Times* drama critic.

❼ Ethel Barrymore Theatre. Named for the actress who was part of the most famous theater family in U.S. history.

❽ Eugene O'Neill Theatre. Named for the only American playwright to win the Nobel Prize for Literature.

❾ Gershwin Theatre. Named for the great composer/lyricist brothers George and Ira Gershwin. Also houses the Theatre Hall of Fame.

❿ Winter Garden Theatre. Named for European "winter gardens" (indoor botanical gardens), and a name shared by theaters in London, Toronto, and Berlin, Germany. Home of the musical *Cats*, the longest-running show in Broadway history.

⓫ Neil Simon Theatre. Named for the playwright who wrote *The Odd Couple* and dozens of other hit plays and movies.

⓬ Ed Sullivan Theater. Current home to *Late Night with David Letterman,* this theater is where the famous Ed Sullivan television show was performed in the 1950s, 1960s, and 1970s.

GLOSSARY

Times Square continues to be a hub of activity.

commerce – the buying and selling of things in order to make money

exclusive – not shared by everyone, doesn't include certain people

foyer – entrance hall, especially of a theater, an apartment building, or a hotel

gridiron – vertical and horizontal framework of right angles

hub – center of activity

Manhattan – an Algonquian Indian word meaning "a place of hills"

notoriety – being widely and unfavorably well known

modest – not large or extreme

millennium – period of one thousand years

mural – painting on a wall

patent – legal document granting the inventor of an item the right to produce or sell the invention

peep show – adult entertainment that is viewed through a small opening and is usually sexually explicit

prostitution – taking part in sexual activity for money

renovate – to restore something to good condition or to make it more modern

The New Amsterdam Theatre is part of Disney's restoration of Times Square.

restoration – work that brings something back to an original condition

unanimously – agreed on by everyone

watt – unit for measuring electrical power

TIMELINE

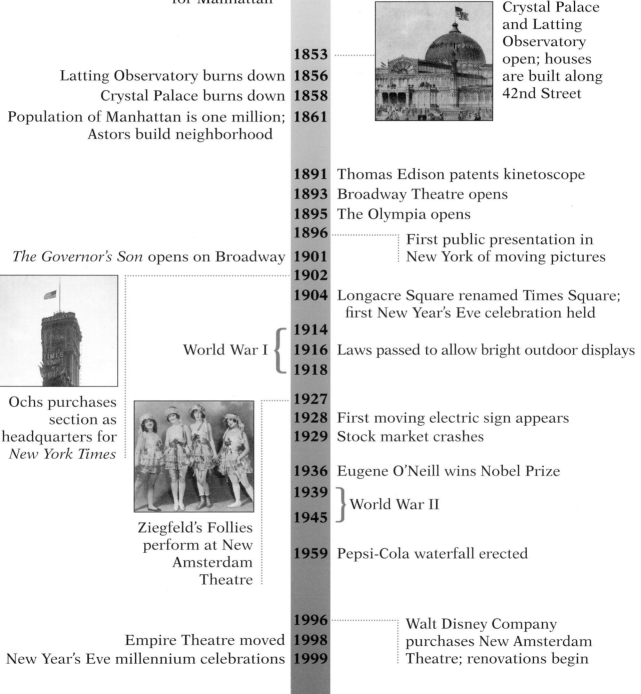

Gridiron street pattern laid out for Manhattan **1811**

1853 Crystal Palace and Latting Observatory open; houses are built along 42nd Street

Latting Observatory burns down **1856**
Crystal Palace burns down **1858**
Population of Manhattan is one million; Astors build neighborhood **1861**

1891 Thomas Edison patents kinetoscope
1893 Broadway Theatre opens
1895 The Olympia opens
1896 First public presentation in New York of moving pictures

The Governor's Son opens on Broadway **1901**
1902
1904 Longacre Square renamed Times Square; first New Year's Eve celebration held

World War I **{** **1914**
1916 Laws passed to allow bright outdoor displays
1918

Ochs purchases section as headquarters for *New York Times*

1927
1928 First moving electric sign appears
1929 Stock market crashes

1936 Eugene O'Neill wins Nobel Prize
1939 **}** World War II
1945

Ziegfeld's Follies perform at New Amsterdam Theatre

1959 Pepsi-Cola waterfall erected

1996 Walt Disney Company purchases New Amsterdam Theatre; renovations begin
Empire Theatre moved **1998**
New Year's Eve millennium celebrations **1999**

DEDICATION
For my father

INDEX (*Boldface* page numbers indicate illustrations.)

PHOTO CREDITS

Photographs ©: AP/Wide World Photos: 27, 30 top (Suzanne Plunkett), 25 (Emile Wamsteker); Archive Photos: cover (Reuters/Peter Morgan), 4, 18, 31 bottom; Bridgeman Art Library International Ltd., London/New York: 6; Brown Brothers: 1, 2, 11, 13, 15, 17 bottom, 20, 31 middle; Corbis-Bettmann: 7, 9; Courtesy of PepsiCo, Inc.: 23; Gamma-Liaison, Inc.: 3 (Jonathan Elderfield); Monkmeyer Press: 24, 26, 30 bottom (Arlene Collins); Museum of the City of New York: 10, 12, 19; New York Public Library Picture Collection: 8, 14, 31 top; Photofest: 16, 17 top, 21.
Maps by TJS Design, Inc.

ABOUT THE AUTHOR

Wende Fazio lives in Elizabeth, New Jersey, with her husband. She received her B.A. from Rutgers University. She is a freelance writer and has written several books on a variety of subjects. This is her fourth book for Children's Press.